C++:

The Ultimate Crash Course to Learning C++ (from basics to advanced)

Copyright © 2017 Paul Laurence

All rights reserved.

ISBN: 1976240476
ISBN-13: 978-1976240478

CONTENTS

Introduction viii

Chapter 1 – Beginning C++ 10

Chapter 2 – Basic Input & Output 29

Chapter 3 – Conditionals 33

Chapter 4 – Working with Arrays 59

Chapter 5 – Pointers 67

Chapter 6 – Functions 71

Chapter 7 – Classes & Objects 78

Chapter 8 – Inheritance 92

Chapter 9 – The New Versions: C++ 11 96

Chapter 10 – The New Versions: C++ 14 123

Conclusion 133

Introduction

If you are reading this book it means that you are taking the initiative to learn C++. C++ was first developed in 1979 by Bjarne Stroustrup. It is a general and efficient programming language that is highly irreplaceable.

C++ is an extension of the C programming language. Bjarne's knowledge of the SIMULA language and its object oriented model aided him in creating class extensions to C. It was originally named C withClasses. It was later renamed to C++.

C++ has a variety of features. These features include:

- C++ is efficient.

- C++ is a static programming language.

- C++ is an object oriented language: The use of objects allows for the division of larger programs into smaller subsets with the use of classes and objects.

- C++ is multi-paradigm: This gives the developers freedom to choose what style of programming they want to use. There are 7 different styles to be chosen from.

- C++ utilizes a standard library: This means that C++ is able to extend the power of its language by utilizing the items with the library.

Learning C++ is something that can take your resume to a new level. It is still used in many major applications, games, browsers and so much more. People are continuously developing and extending upon the functionality of C++. Open source platforms like Github are home to thousands of C++ repositories.

With C++ growing the opportunities for C++ developers are growing as well. Within these positions one can expect an average salary of $100,000 with thousands of jobs being advertised each month.

Although this book is a perfect starting point, don't expect to learn C++ overnight. This language takes practice, persistence and perseverance. If you were wondering, no, you do NOT need to know C before you can grasp C++.

Use the following chapters and exercises as a roadmap on your C++ programming journey, the knowledge awaits.

Chapter 1 – Beginning C++

Before you begin to develop in C++ you must first set up an environment that allows you to do effectively. With this being said, you will need a way to run and compile your C++ programs. This can be done in a plethora of ways.

These ways include the following:

1. Online: Running and compiling programs online is an easy way to avoid excessive downloads or new software. It is also a good option when running programs quickly. There are a good number of sites which allow for this. Due to ease of use, this is the option which will be utilized in this book. Ideoone.com is an excellent option for doing so.

2. Mac OS X: Programs can be run on a MAC operating system using a program called XCode. This can be

downloaded from the Apple developer page. The latest version is highly recommended.

3. Linux: In order to run programs effectively with a Linux machine, you will need to install a compiler. GNU GCC is a recommended compiler for beginners or users new to programming in this operating system. You must also download a text editor. Gedit, being one example.

4. Windows: Being that Windows is a standard and widespread platform there are several options available for use with it. These may include Code::Blocks, JGrasp or Eclipse.

In order to better understand the structure of a C++ program, Hello World will be used as a template. Hello World programs are generally used for beginners in a various programming languages.

The first line of the program is used to include the header file within your program. This allows for you to use the operations included in them. The namespace std is needed in order to accurately reference a variety of operations. It also aids you in not having to write the std in front of every cout statement. This line basically refers to the use of a standard namespace.

```
#include <iostream>
using namespace std;
int main()
{
    cout<<"Hello World!";
    return 0;
}
```

The third line simply refers to this being the main function of your program. The body of the program resides inside of the brackets. The cout statement simply prints the items within the quotes or in some cases variable names. This would depend on what is listed in the cout statement. The last line before the bracket is important because it essentially closes or terminates the program's main function.

If you are familiar with other programming languages, it is easy to understand that all programs are simply a series of ordered instructions or commands for a computer to perform. These instructions are made up of statement. A _statement_ is the smallest unit of a programming language which is equivalent to a sentence in the English language. In C++, a semicolon is used to complete a statement instead of a period. The notion of a variable is also one that is widespread and heavily used when programming. A variable is a name given to a space in memory that can be changed based on the instructions of the program.

Variables can have a variety of types. These types indicate what can be stored within that specific variable. Variable types include:

Integer (int) – This variable type stores only single integers with no decimals. Examples include 5 or 4509. They must be at least 16 bits long. Examples of this include 7854 or 34,

Character (char) – This type refers to a single character, like 'a' and is at least 8 bits long.

float - Stores floating point values such as 3.1555. Is usually 32 bits long.

double - Similar to float but with twice the precision. Is usually 64 bits long.

Boolean (bool) - Stores true/false values.

void - Cannot store data directly, but acts a bit like a placeholder.

Type	Description
bool	Stores either value true or false.
char	Typically a single octet(one byte). This is an integer type.
int	The most natural size of integer for the machine.
float	A single-precision floating point value.
double	A double-precision floating point value.
void	Represents the absence of type.
wchar_t	A wide character type.

Using Variables

A variable is a very fundamental piece of a program. They can be of alphanumeric nomenclature but must always begin with a letter. Variables are used in a variety of statements within a program.

There are 3 types of statements. These types include *declaration statements*, *assignment statements* and *output statements*. Examples of all are provided below.

Before a variable can be used in a program it must first be declared with a declaration statement. A declaration statement gives a name and type to a place in memory where a specific value will be held. In the above example, the name

is y and the type is "double".

```
//Declaration Statement
double y;

//Assignment Statement
y=20.5

//Output Statements
std::cout << y;
```

An *assignment statement* assigns a specific value to a *variable,* y. In the example, y is being assigned a value of 20.

An *output statement* simply prints the value of a specific item or variable. The example above would have an output of 20.

Declaration and assignment of a variable can also take place together; this is referred to as *initialization*. It is important to remember that the only time to initialize a variable is when it is being defined.

```
//initialization Statement
double y = 20.5;
```

Variables may also be declared together using one statement instead of multiples. This can be done by simply following the syntax below.

```
double x,y,z;
```

The above statement simply declares x,y and z all as the type double or decimal numbers.

Practice Questions

Use the practice problems below to ensure that you understand the bare bones of C++ programming.

C++

1. Which of the following is the correct way to write a comment in C++ ?

   a) /*Here is a comment*/

   b) \\Here is another comment\\

   c) //Here is the last comment

2. Hof the options below, which shows a variable declared and initialized correctly, to a value of 10?

   a) int a 10;

   b) int b=10;

   c) double c=10;

3. Of the options below which shows how you would declare a double called number and initialize it to 5?

   a) double number 5;

   b) double number =5

   c) double number =5;

4. Which of the following is the correct way to print an integer named sum to the screen?

   a) cout<<sum<<endl;

   b) cout"sum"<<endl;

c) cout>>sum>>endl;

5. Within a C++ program can multiple data types be declared at once? sum, age, group;

   a) yes

   b) no

6. There are several data types that can be used in C++. What type of information does a data type of double hold?

   a) integers

   b) double integers

   c) decimals

7. What is the correct way to read in input from a user in an int called check?

   a) cout>>"check";

   b) cin>>check;

   c) cin<<check;

8. What is the correct way to read in input from a user in a double called sum?

   a) cin<<sum;

   b) cout>>sum;

c) cin>>sum;

9. For what reason can integers not be divided by themselves?

   a) Their values will be truncated

   b) You will receive an error message instead of the actual answer

   c) your program will break as soon as the statement is hit

Solutions

1. Which of the following is the correct way to write a comment in C++ ?

   a) /*Here is a comment*/

   b) \\Here is another comment\\

   c) //Here is the last comment

2. Of the options below, which shows a variable declared and initialized correctly, to a value of 10?

   a) int a 10;

   b) int b=10;

   c) double c=10;

3. Of the options below which shows how you would declare a double called number and initialize it to 5?

   a) double number 5;

   b) double number =5

   c) double number =5;

4. Which of the following is the correct way to print an integer named sum to the screen?

   a) cout<<sum<<endl;

   b) cout"sum"<<endl;

   c) cout>>sum>>endl;

5. Within a C++ program is it legal to declare multiple integers at one time like the following, int sum,age,group;

   a) yes

   b) no

6. What do double data types hold?

   a) integers

   b) double integers

   c) decimals

7. What is the correct way to read in input from a user in an double called check?

    a) cout>>"check";

    b) cin>>check;

    c) cin<<check;

8. What is the correct way to read in input from a user in a double called sum?

    a) cin<<sum;

    b) cout>>sum;

    c) cin>>sum;

9. Why shouldn't integers be divided by other integers?

    a) The value of the answers will be truncated

    b) You will receive an error message instead of the actual answer

    c) your program will break as soon as the statement is hit

Using Modifiers & Qualifiers

Modifiers can also be used on various types. Modifiers can indicate the sign of a number or provide more detailed information about a variable. Modifiers can be used on **characters**, **integers** and anything of the type **double**. Modifiers are used to manipulate variables into fitting into precise scenarios.

Data type modifier types include:

- Unsigned
- Signed
- Short
- Long

C++

Type	Typical Bit Width	Typical Range
char	1byte	-128 to 127 or 0 to 255
unsigned char	1byte	0 to 255
signed char	1byte	-128 to 127
int	4bytes	-2147483648 to 2147483647
unsigned int	4bytes	0 to 4294967295
signed int	4bytes	-2147483648 to 2147483647
short int	2bytes	-32768 to 32767
unsigned short int	2bytes	0 to 65,535
signed short int	2bytes	-32768 to 32767
long int	8bytes	-9,223,372,036,854,775,808 to 9,223,372,036,854,775,807
signed long int	8bytes	-9,223,372,036,854,775,808 to 9,223,372,036,854,775,807
unsigned long int	8bytes	0 to 18,446,744,073,709,551,615
float	4bytes	+/- 3.4e +/- 38 (~7 digits)
double	8bytes	+/- 1.7e +/- 308 (~15 digits)
long double	8bytes	+/- 1.7e +/- 308 (~15 digits)
wchar_t	2 or 4 bytes	1 wide character

```
unsigned variable_2;
unsigned int variable_1;
```

Run the following program in order to get a better understanding modifiers.

```
#include <iostream>
using namespace std;

/* This program shows the difference between
 * signed and unsigned integers.
 */
int main() {
    short int variable_2;       // a signed short integer
    short unsigned int variable_1; // an unsigned short integer

    variable_1 = 50000;

    variable_2 = variable_1;
    cout << variable_2 << " <-- Variable 1 and Variable 2 --> "
    << variable_1;

    return 0;
}
```

The output of the program is: -15536 <-- Variable 1 and Variable 2 --> 50000. The output found above is due to bit pattern that represents 50,000 as a short unsigned integer is interpreted as -15,536 by a short.

There are 3 types of qualifiers in C++. These include const (constant), volatile and restrict.

<u>Const</u> is used for objects that cannot be changed as your program run. <u>Volatile</u> is the opposite, the value in a variable of this type may be changed throughout the program even in ways not explicitly specified. A pointer with <u>restrict</u> as its qualifier can only be retrieved through said pointer.

Keywords

C++, like many programming languages, also uses a set of keywords. Keywords are words in a language with a special meaning that may not be used in any other way. They are reserved due to their special meaning.

asm	else	new	this
auto	enum	operator	throw
bool	explicit	private	true
break	export	protected	try
case	extern	public	typedef
catch	false	register	typeid
char	float	reinterpret_cast	typename
class	for	return	union
const	friend	short	unsigned
const_cast	goto	signed	using
continue	if	sizeof	virtual
default	inline	static	void
delete	int	static_cast	volatile
do	long	struct	wchar_t
double	mutable	switch	while
dynamic_cast	namespace	template	

Comments

Comments are an important part of any program, they allow the reader or alternate developer to understand the intended purpose of your program and what each line does.

There are two ways to create comments within your code.

```
/* This is a multi-line comment
 * because it can span more than 1 line
 */


//This is a single line comment.
```

C++ Basics Practice

1. What <iostream> known as in programming?
    a) directive
    b) pre-processor directive
    c) file

2. Does using namespace have any significance when coding? Would we still be able to use cout and cin if it was not there?
    a) Yes
    b) No

3. What would be required to print using cout if the namespace is not declared at the beginning of the program?
   a) std::cout<<"Hello";
   b) nothing changes
   c) std:namespace:cout<<"Hello";

4. In int main(), what does the abbreviation int actually stand for?
   a) integrate
   b) It has no value
   c) integer

5. What is the correct way to print to the screen?
   a) cout<<"This is a displayed statement"<<endl;
   b) cout<< ("I can finally program);
   c) cin<<"This is my 18th program of this type<<endl;

6. what does end1 mean/ what does it do?
   a) ends the whole program
   b) goes to a new line
   c) nothing

7. At the end of all C++ programs what number is returned?
   a) 0
   b) 04
   c) 3

Practice Problem Solutions

1. What <iostream> known as in programming?

a) directive
b) pre-processor directive
c) file

2. Does using namespace have any significance when coding? Would we still be able to use cout and cin if it was not there? The answer is the same.
   a) Yes
   b) No

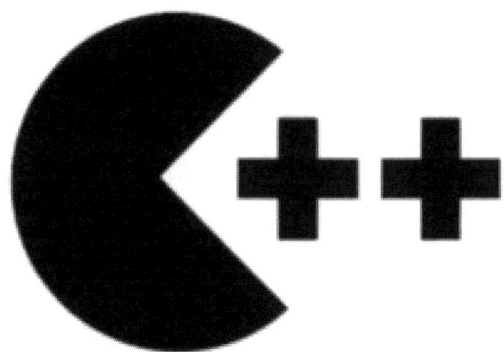

3. What would be required to print using cout if the namespace is not declared at the beginning of the program?
   a) std::cout<<"Hello";
   b) nothing changes
   c) std:namespace:cout<<"Hello";

4. In int main(), what does the abbreviation int actually stand for?
   a) integrate
   b) It has no value
   c) integer

5. What is the correct way to print to the screen?
   a) cout<<"This is a displayed statement"<<endl;
   b) cout<< ("I can finally program);
   c) cin<<"This is my 18th program of this type<<endl;

6. what does endl mean/ what does it do?
   a) ends the whole program
   b) goes to a new line
   c) nothing

7. At the end of all C++ programs what number is returned?
   a) 0
   b) 04
   c) 3

Chapter 2 – Basic Input & Output

One of the most common functions of programming is input and output. Within C++ input and output occur in streams. Streams are also known as sequences of bytes.

If the given bytes originate from a keyboard or a disk drive and flow to the main memory, this is categorized as an input operation. Output is categorized as the flow of bytes from the main memory to a screen or monitor.

The header file line in the program is essential to input and ouput. The line, <iostream> in the beginning of the program is the header file which defines the input and output objects.

Other header file types include <iomanip> and <fstream>.

Using cout

The cout object is an instance of the ostream class, which is connected to the output device or monitor. This is a fairly simply command and is most times used in conjunction with cin although it can be used without it.

Run the program below in order to accurately see the cout statement at work.

```
#include <iostream>

using namespace std;

int main( ) {
    int a = 67;
    int b = 67;
    int c = a+b;

    cout << "Value of c is : " << c << endl;
}
```

The output for the above program should be the correct value of c, with the given statement.

Two important things to note in this program include the insert operator, << and the endl. The endl is used to add a new line to the end of the given string line. The << can be used multiple times, as we can see above.

Using cin

The use of cin allows the user to input information into a given variable. This object belongs to the istream family, which is attached to the input device which is generally a device similar to a keyboard. The extraction operator is the opposite of the insertion operator. It is simply >>, which will be seen in the program example below.

```cpp
#include <iostream>

using namespace std;
int main( ) {
   char petname[40];
   char yourname[60];
   cout << "Please enter the name of your pet: ";
   cin >> petname;
   cout << "Your name is: " << petname << endl;
   cout << "Please enter your full name: ";
   cin >> yourname;
   cout << "Your name is: " << yourname << endl;
}
```

Upon running the program, you will be prompted to enter in your pet's name. It will then be printed. You will then be prompted to enter your name and it will be printed as well.

Try this exercise on your own for more input and output practice.

1. Answer the prompt below so that the input amounts are 23, 55.7 and 12.

```
#include <iostream>

using namespace std;

int main( ) {
    int X, Y;
    double Z;

    cin >> X;
    cin >> Y;
    cin >> Z;
    cout << " X" << X << endl;

}
```

Chapter 3 – Conditionals

Another major component in C++ programming is the use of conditionals. Conditionals are statements that cause a program to alter its intended path based on a program's current value. One of the first and most basic conditional statements to be discussed is an *if* statement.

Before going into various types of conditional statements we must first know which relational operands to use within our statements and what they mean.

>	Greater Than	8 > 6 TRUE
<	Less Than	1 < 9 TRUE
>=	Greater Than or Equal	3 >= 0 TRUE
<=	less than or equal	6 <= 10 TRUE
==	equal to	6 == 6 TRUE
!=	not equal to	7 != 3 TRUE
&&		AND
||		OR
!		NOT

Using If Statements

In order to fully understand if statements within C++ you must first understand how they function

The structure of an if statement is as follows:

```
if (TRUE)
{
```

Perform the next statement

}

---

if (TRUE)
{
   Perform this block of statements if True
}
else
{
   Perform this block of statement if False
}

In the first example, if the given expression is true, the statement will implement. However, in the second statement, if the statement is true, the statement will execute but if the statement is false, the else statement will execute.

The following program will demonstrate how if statements operate and execute.

```cpp
#include <iostream>

int main()
{
    std::cout << "Enter a digit between 1 and 10: ";
    int num;
    std::cin >> num;

    if (num > 10)
        std::cout << num << "Your number is greater than 10\n";
    else
        std::cout << num << " Your number is not greater than 10\n";

    return 0;
}
```

As you may have guessed, there will also be times when more than one if statement is needed. Therefore, multiple if statements can be used.

The example program below shows how multiple if statements execute. In order to successfully execute multiple if statements we can use a block.

```cpp
#include <iostream>

int main()
{
    std::cout << "Enter a number: ";
    int x;
    std::cin >> x;

    if (x > 10)
        {
        // both statements will be executed if x > 10
        std::cout << "You entered " << x << "\n";
        std::cout << x << "is greater than 10\n";
        }
    else
        {
        // both statements will be executed if x <= 10
        std::cout << "You entered " << x << "\n";
```

Blocks are essentially the use of the brackets {}. Using these brackets allows the user to tell program where to start and end an if statement. In the event that the blocks are not specified the program is smart enough to implicitly define blocks.

If statements can also be chained together by using *else if* as shown in the program below.

Aside from the ability to input chained if statements, nesting if statements are also very possible to do in C++. The following is an example of nesting functions.

The above code is confusing simply because of the missing brackets. Adding blocks around the else would make the code clearer. This ambiguity is known as a <u>dangling else.</u>

```
#include <iostream>

int main()
{
    std::cout << "Please input a digit: ";
    int num;
    std::cin >> num;

    if (num > 10)
        std::cout << num<< "Your number is far greater than 10\n";
    else if (num < 10)
        std::cout << num << "The entered number is far less than 10\n";
    else
        std::cout << num << "Your number is 10!\n";
```

```
#include <iostream>

int main()
{
    std::cout << "Entera random digit: ";
    int num;
    std::cin >> num;

    if (num > 10) // outer if statement
        // it is bad coding style to nest if statements this way
        if (num < 20) // inner if statement
            std::cout << num << " Your number is between the numbers 10 and 20\n";

        // Which If statement corresponds to the else listed below?
        else
            std::cout << num << "Woah! Your number is far greater than 20\n";

    return 0;
```

Still confused on how to implement an if or if-else statement. Use the questions below as practice.

1. Which of the following provide the correct structure for an if statement?
   A. if *this* then that
   B. if { *expression}*
   C. if (*expression*)
   D. else *expression* if

2. Write a program that allows the user to input a number into the system. The program should then tell the user 2 separate statements if the number is greater than or less than 50. This will be done using input and condition statements. If the number is greater than 50 the program should print, "Wow, this number is big". If the number is less than 50 the program should print, "Yikes, this number is too small".

3. If x is equal to 10 and y is equal to 30 will this condition execute? if(x > y)

   a) yes

   b) no

4. What do conditions do for programs?

   a) improves processing

   b) adds flexibility to a program while lessening it's length

   c) breaks them

5. What does an else statement do?

   a) gives an alternative route to the given conditions

   b) never executes

   c) it looks good in the program

6. What do the following condition mean within the context of a conditional? if (a!=b)

    a) a is equal to b

    b) checks if a does not equal b

    c) None of the above are true

7. In an if statement when do you need the curly braces?

    a) always

    b) generally they should be used where there are 2 or more lines in the condition statement.

    c) never

8. What does the following condition mean in plain English? if (y!=x)

    a) if y doesn't equal x

    b) if x doesn't equal y

    c) if x is less than y

9. If a is equivalent to 20 and b is equivalent ti 20 will this condition execute? if (a!=b)

    a) yes

    b) no

10. What does the following statement mean? if (a==b)

    a) if a is greater than b

    b) if a is equal to b

    c) if b is greater than or equal to a

11. If x is equivalent to 20 and y is equals to 8 is the following condition abled to be executed? if(x<=y)

    a) yes

    b) no

Solutions

1. C.

2. #include <iostream>

   using namespace std;

   int main()
   {
   cout << "Enter your number " << endl;

   int number;

```
cin >> number;

if(value < 50)
{
    cout << "Yikes, this number is too small";
}
else
{
    cout << "Wow, this number is big.";
}

return 0;
}
```

3.. If x is equal to 10 and y is equal to 30 will this condition execute? if(x > y)

a) yes

b) no

4. What do conditions do for programs?

a) improves processing

b) adds flexibility to a program while lessening its length

c) breaks them

5. What does an else statement do?

a) gives an alternative route to the given conditions

b) never executes

c) it looks good in the program

6. What do the following condition mean within the context of a conditional? if (a!=b)

a) a is equal to b

b) checks if a does not equal b

c) None of the above are true

7. In an if statement when do you need the curly braces?

a) always

b) generally they should be used where there are 2 or more lines in the condition statement.

c) never

8. What does the following condition mean in plain English? if (y!=x)

a) if y doesn't equal x

b) if x doesn't equal y

c) if x is less than y

9. If a is equivalent to 20 and b is equivalent to 20 will this condition execute? if (a!=b)

a) yes

b) no

10. What does the following statement mean? if (a==b)

a) if a is greater than b

b) if a is equal to b

c) if b is greater than or equal to a

11. If x is equivalent to 20 and y is equals to 8 is the following condition abled to be executed? if(x<=y)

a) yes

b) no

Loops

Aside from conditional statements, loops are utilized when parts of code need to be repeated. Instead of rewriting or copying sections of code, loops are used. Loops allow a user to repeat certain portions of code over and over until its completion.

The simplest loop which exists in a C++ program is the *for* loop. The syntax for a for loop is as follows:

---

for (variable initialization; condition; variable update) {

  Statements to be executed as long as condition, in parentheses is true.

}

Loops utilize 2 operands you must be familiar with in order to progress any further. These are the increment and decrement symbols(++ & --).

In order to further break down the structure of a for loop, see the example below.

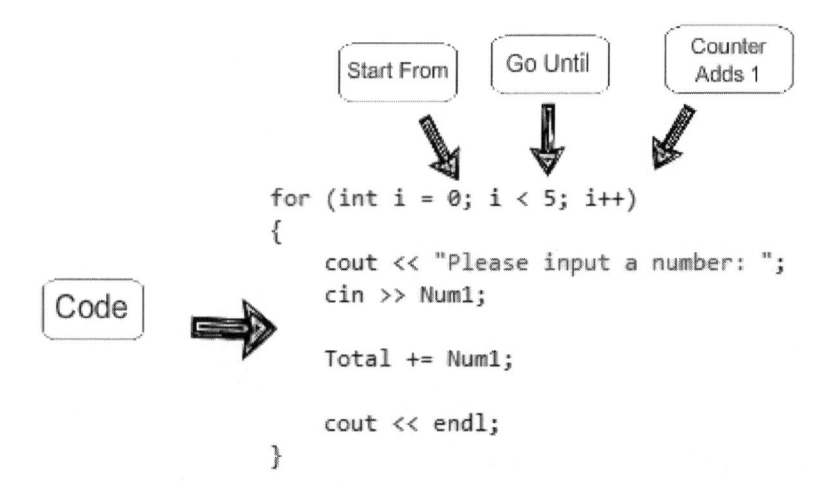

```
for (int i = 0; i < 5; i++)
{
    cout << "Please input a number: ";
    cin >> Num1;

    Total += Num1;

    cout << endl;
}
```

The code in the for loop above will execute until the counter variable reaches 4. Once the variable reaches 5, it will no longer execute since it will not meet the for loop condition.

Another loop type which is frequently used is *while* loop. The while loop continuously executes a block of statements as long as the while's test statement is true.

```cpp
#include <iostream>
using namespace std;

int main ()
{
  for (int m=10; m>0; m--) {
    cout << m << ", ";
  }
  cout << "The End!\n";
}
```

Execute the following code to see a for loop in action.

This for loop will have the following output:

```
10, 9, 8, 7, 6, 5, 4, 3, 2, 1, The End!
```

The following diagram shows how a while loop operates.

```
                    │
                    ▼
              ╱Test    ╲    false
              ╲expression╱ ─────────┐
                    │               │
                    │ true          │
                    ▼               │
            ┌───────────────┐       │
            │ Body of while │       │
            │     Loop      │       │
            └───────────────┘       │
                                    ▼
                           ┌─────────────────┐
                           │ Statement just  │
                           │   below while   │
                           └─────────────────┘
                                    │
                                    ▼
```

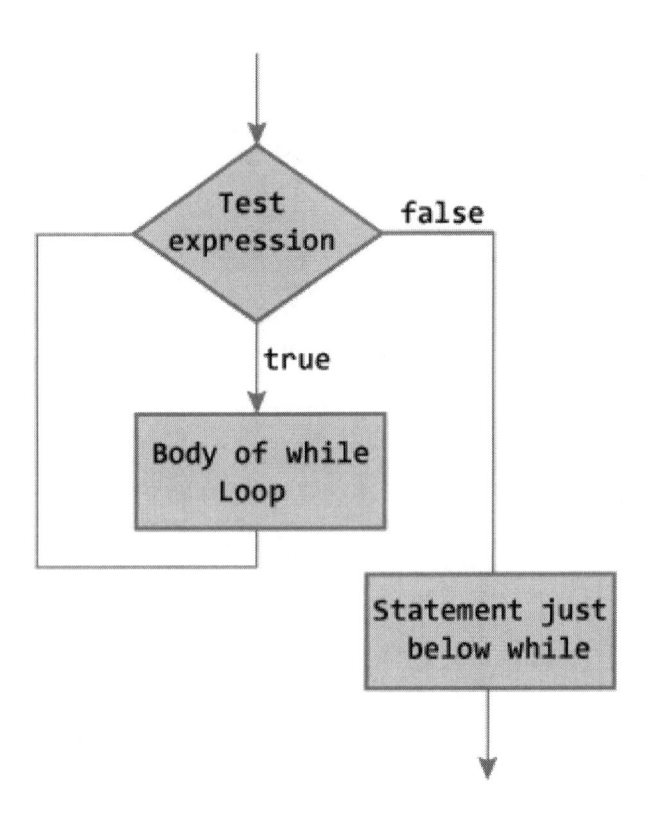

Figure: Flowchart of while Loop

The test expression can be any combination of Boolean expressions. However, as long as that statement is true the body of the loop will execute.

The syntax for a while loop is as follows:

```
while ( w < 25 ) { // While w is less than 25
    cout<< w <<endl;
    w++;        // Revise w so the condition can be met
}
```

One loop which is similar to the while loop is the *do while* loop. The do while loop, although similar to the while loop checks the condition after the execution of the given statement. When something needs to be completed at least once a do while loop will be used. The syntax for a do while loop is as follows:

```
do {

} while ( condition );
```

It is important to note that while the condition remains true, the statements within the do will continue to implement. It is also important to remember that the do while must be ended with a semi-colon, also known as a trailing semi colon.

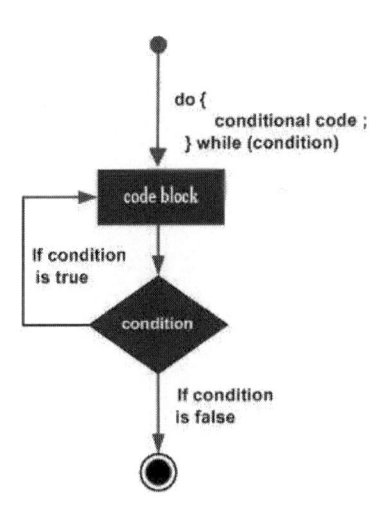

The above diagram is a graphical reference of how do while loops operate. Execute the following code in order to see a do while loop in action.

```
#include <iostream>
using namespace std;
int main () {
   // Local variable declaration:
   int b = 0;
   // do loop execution
   do {
      cout << "The value of b is: " << b << endl;
      b = b + 2;
   }while( a < 20 );
   return 0;
}
```

Use the following practice problems to further your knowledge of loops.

1. What will the following code print?
   ```
   var x = 0;
   while (x < 3) {
   println("bye");
      x++;
   }
   ```

2. What will the following code print?
   ```
   var x = 0;
   while (x < 3) {
      println("hi");
      x++;
   }
   println("bye");
   ```

3. What will the following code print?
   ```
   var y = 0;
   while (y < 0) {
      println("hi");
   }
   ```

4. Which for loop will not work?
   a) for (i=0; i<5; i++)
   b) for (i=5; i<=10; i++)
   c) for (i=5; i=10; i++)

5. What type of loop will execute at least once?

Practice Question Solutions:

1. bye
   bye
   bye

2. hi
   hi
   hi
   bye

3. This code will not print anything because y is equal to zero and it can therefore never be less than zero.

4. C.

5. A do while loop will execute at least once.

Break & Continue Statements

The break and continue statements alter the usual flow of a program. A break statement concludes a loop and a switch statement, which will be covered later, immediately when it appears.

A break statement works with while, do while and for loops. The image below shows how a break operates in each loop type.

C++

```
while (test expression) {              do {
    statement/s                            statement/s
    if (test expression) {                 if (test expression) {
        break;                                 break;
    }                                      }
    statement/s                            statement/s
}                                      }
                                       while (test expression);
```

```
for (intial expression; test expression; update expression) {
    statement/s
    if (test expression) {
        break;
    }
    statements/
}
```

NOTE: The break statment may also be used inside body of else statement.

The continue statement is used to skip certain conditions within a loop. This statement is used within a condition statement. The diagram below illustrates how a continue statement operates.

```
while (test expression) {              do {
    statement/s                            statement/s
    if (test expression) {                 if (test expression) {
        continue;                              continue;
    }                                      }
    statement/s                            statement/s
}                                      }
                                       while (test expression);
```

```
for (intial expression; test expression; update expression) {
    statement/s
    if (test expression) {
        continue;
    }
    statements/
}
```

NOTE: The continue statment may also be used inside body of else statement.

Run the following program to see how a continue statement operates in code.

```cpp
#include <iostream>
using namespace std;
int main()
{
   for (int j = 1; j <= 10; ++j)
   {
      if ( j == 6 || j == 9)
      {
         continue;
      }
      cout << j << "\t";
   }
   return 0;
}
```

Switch Statements

Switch statements are used when multiple if else statements are needed. Switch statements usually execute faster than multiple nested if statements. They are also easier to comprehend and program.

The syntax of a switch statement is as follows:

```
switch (n)

{

    case constant1:

        // code to be executed if n is equal to constant1;

        break;

    case constant2:

        // code to be executed if n is equal to constant2;

        break;

    default:

        // code to be executed if n doesn't match any constant

}
```

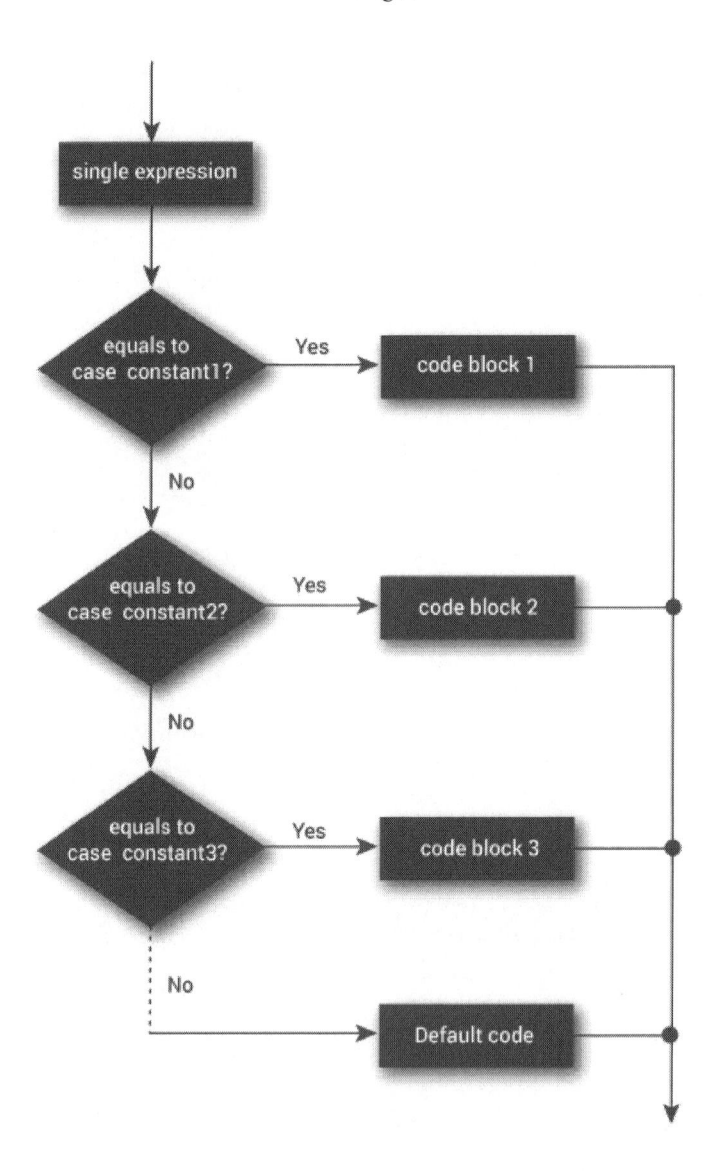

The above syntax and diagram show that when a case constant is located which matches n, the program's control passes to the associated case block. A block of code will be implemented until the program reaches the break statement or it is the end of a block.

C++

Practice with Switch Statements

Use these questions to practice with switch statements and their uses.

1. Write a program that determines a student's letter grade based on their numerical grade. The program should output the letter grade for the student. The switch should determine if the grade is an A, B, C, D or F.
2. There is something specific that comes after every case in a switch. What is that item?
3. Is it legal for cases to contain condition statements?
4. Explain what is incorrect about the following case. case (x > 3):
5. Explain what is wrong with the following case. case 3:
6. Should a case always have curly brace? True or False.

Solutions

1. switch (grade)   {

    case(1):
        if   (numAvg   <   60)
        grade   =   'F';
        break;

    case(2):
        if   (numAvg   <   70)
        grade   =   'D';
        break;

    case(3):
        if   (grade   <   80)
        grade   =   'C';
        break;

case(4):

if (grade < 90) grade = 'B';
break;

default: grade = 'A';

2. C. Break
3. No, switches cannot have conditions
4. This is wrong because a case cannot have a condition.
5. Nothing is wrong with this statement.
6. False.

Chapter 4 – Working with Arrays

Arrays are extremely useful for not only storing data under a single variable name but also for storing elements in an ordered list format. They are ultimately used to organize large amounts of data and information. When attempting to iterate through an array loops are a highly useful tool for assigning values and for printing them out.

In a situation where you have multiple variable like the one listed below, it would be easier to simply use an array. The information below simply shows the ages of 5 different people.

int Person1=15;

int Person2=24;

int Person3=54;

int Person4=33;

int Person5=120;

Instead of declaring each person as a different variable it would be easier to simply declare an array of 5 with various people's ages.

The declaration of this array would be the following: *int person_ages [5];*

```
int person_ages [5];
```

The array type would be int, this is the type of the information that would be being stored. The second item is simply the array name. In this case the name is person_ages. The last piece within the brackets holds the amount of items in your array.

Initializing Arrays

There are two ways to initialize an array. The first way is to simply list the array position and set the value. This is done, as shown below.

```
person_age[0]=43;
person_age[1]=49;
```

```
person_age[2]=5;
person_age[3]=10;
person_age[4]=70;
```

When manually setting the values in the array you also have the option to set them as shown below.

```
//initialize
person_age = {43,49,5,10,70};
```

Although manually setting an array may be okay for an array with 5 items. What do you do when your array has 500 items? This is where the use of a for loop would come in. Using a loop is more efficient and much less work although it works the same way. The example below uses a for loop to iterate through an array for the purpose of printing, although the same can be implemented for initializing depending on the function of your code.

```
#include <iostream>

using namespace std;

int main()
{
    int a;//a is your counter variable
    int person_age [5];
    ages={45,24,5,95,12};

    for (a=0; a<5; a++)//set 'a' to 0
execute while 'a' is less than 5
        {
            cout<<person_age[a]<<endl;
        }

    return 0;
}
```

Run the above program in your environment to see it in action and see what it prints.

The example below shows how you can use for loops in order to iterate through the initialization of your array instead of setting it manually.

```
#include <iostream>

using namespace std;

int main()
{
    int a;
    int person_ages [5];

        for (a=0; a<5; a++)
        {
            cout<<"Enter    ther    person's age"<<endl;
            cin>>ages[a];
        }

    for (a=0; a<5; a++)
        {
            cout<<ages[a]<<endl;
        }

return 0;
}
```

Practice with Arrays

Use these question in order to practice with arrays and gain a better understanding of applying the concept.

1. From the options below, how is an array declared?
    a) this_array [15];
    b) this_array (15);
    c) this_array {15};

2. What is the general purpose of an array? What do they do?
    a) The purpose of an array is to hold addresses
    b) The purpose of an array is to hold values under a single name
    c) The purpose of an array is to hold one value

3. double test [8]; What is the name of the array which is declared here?
    a) the data type double
    b) the array does not have a name
    c) test

4. Refer back to question 3. How many values does the test array hold?
    a) It holds 7.
    b) It holds 8
    c) The array holds 6

5. Refer to question 3. By looking at the array declaration, what will the greatest index value be?
    a) The greatest value will be 7.
    b) The greatest value will be 6

c) The greatest value will be 8

6. From the given options, which of the following options shows the correct way to initialize values in an array?
    a) sample_array [15] = (5,3,4,2,7);
    b) sample_array [15] = {5;3;4;2;7};
    c) sample_array [15] = {5,3,4,2,7};

7. Refer to question 6. What is the value in the space located at this_array [3]?
    a) The value is 7
    b) The value is 3
    c) The value is 4

8. Is there a way for an entire array be printed out all at once?
    a) yes
    b) no

9. What must be used when attempting to print out or assign items in an array?
    a) pointers

b) conditions

c) loops

Practice Question Solutions

1. From the options below, how is an array declared?
    a) this_array [15];
    b) ths_array (15);
    c) this_array {15};

2. What is the general purpose of an array? What do they do?
    a) hold addresses
    b) hold values under a single name
    c) hold one value

3. double number [8]; What is the name of the array which is declared here?
    a) double
    b) the array does not have a name
    c) test

4. From question 3, how many values does the declared array hold?
    a) 7
    b) 8
    c) 6

5. From question 3, what will be the greatest index number of the array?
   a) 7
   b) 6
   c) 8

6. From the given options, which of the following options shows the correct way to initialize values in an array?
   a) sample_array [5] = (5,3,4,2,7);
   b) sample_array [5] = {5;3;4;2;7};
   c) sample_array [5] = {5,3,4,2,7};

7. From question 6, provide the value for the item in this_array [3]?
   a) 7
   b) 3
   c) 4

8. Is there a way for an entire array be printed out all at once?
   a) yes
   b) no

9. What must be used when attempting to print out or assign items in an array?
   a) pointers
   b) conditions
   c) loops

Chapter 5 – Pointers

Pointer make certain complex tasks easier and they are fairly simple to use. A pointer is defined as a variable that holds the address of another variable. Much like a variable, before its use it must be defined.

```
type *var-name;
```

When using a pointer, the type is whatever the type of the base type is. For example, if my pointer is pointing to a double variable, my pointer must be a double. The var-name is the name of your pointer. The asterisk must be used in order to denote a pointer.

```
int    *int_point;   // pointer to an integer
double *dou_point;   // pointer to a double
float  *flo_point;   // pointer to a float
char   *ch_point;    // pointer to character
```

The following example shows the information which is

stored in a pointer, run the following code to get a better understanding of pointers.

```cpp
#include <iostream>

using namespace std;

int main () {
    int variable = 10;   // actual variable declaration.
    int *ipointer;       // pointer variable

    cout << "Value of variable: ";
    cout        <<           variable           <<           endl;

    // access the value at the address available in pointer
    cout << "Value of *ipointer variable: ";
    cout << *ipointer << endl;

    return 0;
}
```

Null Pointers

A pointer that is assigned to NULL is referred to as a **null pointer**. A null pointer is assigned at the time of declaration. The null pointer is generally constant and holds a value of zero.

Pointer Math

Being that pointers hold values for numbers, they also have

the ability to perform basic arithmetic functions.

In some programs the developer may choose to use a pointer instead of an array. This is in part because pointers can be incremented and arrays can't, without the help of a loop.

The following program shows how to successfully increment the variable pointer to access each succeeding element of an array:

```cpp
#include <iostream>
using namespace std;
const int MAX = 4;
int main () {
   int  var[MAX] = {10, 100, 200, 300};
   int *ptr;
   // let us have array address in pointer.
   ptr = var;
   for (int j = 0; j < MAX; j++) {
      cout << "Value of var[" << j << "] = ";
      cout << *ptr << endl;
      // point to the next location
      ptr++;
   }

   return 0;
}
```

Being that pointers can be incremented, they can also be

decremented. Run the following code to show how a pointer is decremented.

```
#include <iostream>

using namespace std;
const int MAX = 4;
int main () {
    int  var[MAX] = {10, 100, 200,300};
    int  *ptr;

    ptr = &var[MAX-1];
    for (int j = MAX; j > 0; j--) {
        cout << "Value of var[" << j << "] = ";
        cout << *ptr << endl;

        // point to the previous location
        ptr--;
    }

    return 0;
}
```

Aside from incrementing and decrementing, pointers also have the ability to be compared using relational operators. This includes operators such as ==, <, and >.

Chapter 6 – Functions

Functions are extremely useful sections of code that are written in order accomplish a specific task. When they are used together they create a more sophisticated and clean program.

The basic structure of a function is shown below. Please, note that a prototype is another way of saying or classifying a declaration of a function.

```
return type name (data type variable, data type variable....)
```

Return type: The return type refers to what your function will return after it has completed. For example, if I am creating a program to give me the average age of college students I would use an int because I do not want nor need the decimal places. Therefore, truncation is okay. My return type would then be an int.

Name: This is simply the name of the function. Using the same example, I could name this function *average_age*.

Data type: The data type simply refers to a variable. These are the items that the function can take in to use. It can be one or it can be multiples.

The beginning of the function would look like the sample below.

```
int average_age(int x, int y)
```

The placement of the prototype is shown in the sample below.

```
#include <iostream>
int average_age (int x, int y);

int main()
{
      //main program

return 0;
}

double mult (int x, int y) //notice no semicolon
{
      //function will be written here

}
```

Run the following program as a sample in order to see how functions operate. The function in the following program is used to add two variables and return the sum of them both.

```
//Full working program
#include <iostream>
double summation (int a, int b); // prototype

int main()
{
      int x,y;
      int c;
```

```
        cin>>x;   //the user inputs a value for x
        cin>>y;   //the user inputs a value for y

        c = summation(x,y);   //call the function
summation and pass through the variables you have
read in

        cout<<"The sum of the 2 numbers is "<<c<<endl;

return 0;
}

double summation (int a, int b)   //defining the
function
{
        double z;

        //'a' holds the value of 'x' and 'b' holds the
value of 'y'

        z = a+b;
        return z;   //returns the value of 'z' to the
variable 'c' in main

}
```

Aside from functions that return numbers or variables, there are also functions that do not return anything. These are void functions.

void sum (int x)

This simply means that there will be no values returned as was shown in the last example.

Practicing with Functions

1. When you are using a function, what is the first thing that you have to do?
    a) declare variables
    b) prototype
    c) initialize

2. Where does the prototype fall within your program?
    a) before int main()
    b) before and after int main()
    c) the end of the program

3. Given the example shown, int books (int y), what is the name of the function that was created?
    a) int
    b) int y
    c) books

4. From the example given in question 3, what data type will the function return?
   a) int
   b) string
   c) double

5. From the example given in question 3, what data type will this function take in?
   a) char
   b) String
   c) int

6. char my_function (int a), what type of data will this functions take in?
   a) double
   b) char & double
   c) int

7. Given the function listed, double summation (double a, double b), what is the correct way that you should be calling this function from the main program?
   a) summation (x)
   b) summation (y)
   c) summation (x,y)

8. If you have a variable which is declared within a function, what kind of variable is this?
   a) global variable
   b) local variable
   c) extended variable

9. If we have a function double go (double b), are we able to send it a different variable in the main program or does it have to be b. For example, go (x)
   a) yes
   b) no

Practicing with Function Solutions

1. When you are using a function, what is the first thing that you have to do?
   a) declare variables
   b) prototype
   c) initialize

2. Where does the prototype fall within your program?
   a) before int main()
   b) before and after int main()
   c) the end of the program

3. Given the example shown, int books (int y), what is the name of the function that was created?
   a) int
   b) int y
   c) books

4. From the example given in question 3, what data type will the function return?
   a) int
   b) string
   c) double

5. From the example given in question 3, what data type will this function take in?
   a) char
   b) String
   c) int

6. char my_function (int a), what type of data will this functions take in?
   a) double
   b) char & double
   c) int

7. Given the function listed, double summation (double a, double b), what is the correct way that you should be calling this function from the main program?
   a) summation (a)
   b) summation (a,b)
   c) summation (b)

8. If you have a variable which is declared within a function, what kind of variable is this?
   a) global variable
   b) local variable
   c) extended variable

9. If we have a function double go (double b), are we able to send it a different variable in the main program or does it have to be b. For example, go (x)
   a) yes
   b) no

Chapter 7 – Classes & Objects

One of the main functions of C++ is the addition of object orientation to the C language. Due to this, classes one of the features involved in C++ program. These are referred to at times as user defined types.

Why are Classes Used?

Classes are used in order to detail the structure of an object. It also encompasses the methods which are needed to manipulate the object and any of its characteristics. The functions and data within a class are referred to as its members.

C++ Class Definitions

In reality, a class does not define any type of formal data. It is simply an outline or a blueprint. The class defines the meaning of the class name as well the components of the object it represents. It also defines what operations can be performed by the object.

When defining a class, you must always start with the keyword, **class**. This should be immediately followed by the name of the class. The class body should then follow and all must be enclosed by curly brackets. The class definition must then be followed by a semi colon or list of declaration depending on the user's needs. The following is an example of class declarations.

```
class Person {
    public:
        double weight;  // weight of a person
        double height;  // height in inches of a person
        int age;        // age of a person
};
```

Shown above, you will see the use of the keyword **public**. This is used to determine the level of access the members of the class will have. Anything marked as public can be accessed from anywhere outside of the class but still within the scope of the class object. Public is not the only access method. Things may also be described as ***private***, or ***protected***, which will be discussed later in the chapter.

Define C++ Objects

Since a class is said to be the blueprint for an object, it makes sense that objects are created from classes. Objects are declared the same way that we would declare a variable. Find below the definitions of the person object which was started in the previous section.

```
Person Person1;     // Declare Person1 of type Person
Person Person2;     // Declare Person2 of type Person
```

Both of the objects Person1 and Person2 will have their own copy of data members.

Accessing the Data Members

Any data member of a public access type may be used by simply using (.). This is the access operator.

```cpp
#include <iostream>

using namespace std;

class Person {
   public:
       double weight;   // weight of a person
       double height;   // height in inches of a person
       int age;         // age of a person
};

int main( ) {
     Person Person1;          // Declare Person1 of type Person
     Person Person2;          // Declare Person2 of type Person
    double bmi =0.0

   // Person 1 specification
   Person1.weight= 60.0;
   Person1.height= 30.0;
   Person1.age= 7.0;

   // Person 2 specification
   Person2.weight= 300.0;
   Person2.height= 80.0;
   Person2.age= 30.0;


   // bmi of Person1
   bmi= (Person1.weight*703)/(Person1.height *  Person1.height);
   cout << "BMI of Person1: " << bmi<<endl;

   // volume of box 2
   bmi= (Person2.weight*703)/(Person2.height *  Person2.height);
   cout << "BMI of Person2: " << bmi<<endl;


   return 0;
}
```

Run the program above to see how the access operator is used and how to correctly use objects. Please remember that items which are *private* and *protected* members cannot be accessed using the access operator (.).

The information provided above is simply a basic overview of objects and classes. There are several concepts to review in depth.

Class Member Functions

Member functions operate on objects of a class. It is function that has its definition within the class definition. Aside from within the class definition, member functions can also be defined separately when the **scope resolution operator,::.** This would be declaring the function **inline**.

The above examples are shown below.

```
class Box {
    public:
        double length;      // Length of a box
        double breadth;     // Breadth of a box
        double height;      // Height of a box

        double getVolume(void) {
            return length * breadth * height;
        }
};
```

```
double Box::getVolume(void) {
    return length * breadth * height;
}
```

Class Member Modifiers

Public, **private** and **protected** provide access restrictions to varies class members within the class body. These keywords can be called specifiers. A class has the ability to have multiple blocks of varying access levels. Members and classes, by default, have an access type of *private*.

```
class Base {
    public:
    // public members go here
    protected:
    // protected members go here
    private:
    // private members go here
};
```

Constructors & Deconstructors

A **constructor** is a function of a class that gets implemented whenever new objects are created. They have the same name as the class but do not have any return or void. The example below shows how constructors are used.

```cpp
#include <iostream>

using namespace std;

class Line {
   public:
      void setLength( double len );
      double getLength( void );
      Line();   // This is the constructor

   private:
      double length;
};

// Member functions definitions including constructor
Line::Line(void) {
   cout << "Object is being created" << endl;
}

void Line::setLength( double len ) {
   length = len;
}

double Line::getLength( void ) {
   return length;
}

// Main function for the program
int main( ) {
   Line line;

   // set line length
   line.setLength(6.0);
   cout << "Length of line : " << line.getLength() <<endl;

   return 0;
}
```

Although a constructor generally does not have parameters, it still has the ability to. This aids you in assigning values at the time of object creation. An example of a *parameterized constructor* is shown below.

```cpp
#include <iostream>

using namespace std;

class Line {
   public:
      void setLength( double len );
      double getLength( void );
      Line(double len);    // This is the constructor

   private:
      double length;
};

// Member functions definitions including constructor
Line::Line( double len) {
   cout << "Object is being created, length = " << len << endl;
   length = len;
}

void Line::setLength( double len ) {
   length = len;
}

double Line::getLength( void ) {
   return length;
}

// Main function for the program
int main( ) {
   Line line(10.0);

   // get initially set length.
   cout << "Length of line : " << line.getLength() <<endl;

   // set line length again
   line.setLength(6.0);
   cout << "Length of line : " << line.getLength() <<endl;

   return 0;
}
```

A **deconstructor** is executed when an object goes out of scope. It is also executed when the delete expression is applied to a pointer to the object.

A deconstructor has the same name as the class but is prefixed with a tilde. It can not return or take parameters. It is useful when releasing resources. The following is an example of a deconstructor.

```cpp
#include <iostream>

using namespace std;

class Line {
    public:
        void setLength( double len );
        double getLength( void );
        Line();    // This is the constructor declaration
        ~Line();   // This is the destructor: declaration

    private:
        double length;
};

// Member functions definitions including constructor
Line::Line(void) {
    cout << "Object is being created" << endl;
}

Line::~Line(void) {
    cout << "Object is being deleted" << endl;
}

void Line::setLength( double len ) {
    length = len;
}

double Line::getLength( void ) {
    return length;
}

// Main function for the program
int main( ) {
    Line line;

    // set line length
    line.setLength(6.0);
    cout << "Length of line : " << line.getLength() <<endl;

    return 0;
}
```

Friend Functions

A friend function is defined outside of the scope of the class, however, it is able access all private and protected members. Member functions can not be friend functions. In order to declare a function as a friend, the function must be preceded by the keyword friend. The example below shows how friend functions are used.

```cpp
#include <iostream>

using namespace std;

class Box {
   double width;
public:
   friend void printWidth( Box box );
   void setWidth( double wid );
};

// Member function definition
void Box::setWidth( double wid ) {
   width = wid;
}

// Note: printWidth() is not a member function of any class.
void printWidth( Box box ) {
   /* Because printWidth() is a friend of Box, it can
   directly access any member of this class */
   cout << "Width of box : " << box.width <<endl;
}

// Main function for the program
int main( ) {
   Box box;

   // set box width with member function
   box.setWidth(10.0);

   // Use friend function to print the wdith.
   printWidth( box );

   return 0;
}
```

Static Class Members

Static class members are defined using the keyword **static**. This means that no matter how many object may exist there is only one copy of the static class member.

The following example shows how static class members are used.

A static member function may be called even when no objects of the class exist. It is important to remember that

static functions are accessed by simply using the class name and the scope resolution operator ::. A static member function is only able to access a static data member, static member functions and any other functions from outside the class.

Static data members, static member functions and any other functions from outside the class can be accessed by a static member function. It can also be used to determine if objects have not been created or if they have.

The following is an example of using static function members.

C++

```cpp
#include <iostream>

using namespace std;

class Box {
   public:
      static int objectCount;
      // Constructor definition
      Box(double l = 2.0, double b = 2.0, double h = 2.0) {
         cout <<"Constructor called." << endl;
         length = l;
         breadth = b;
         height = h;
         // Increase every time object is created
         objectCount++;
      }

      double Volume() {
         return length * breadth * height;
      }

      static int getCount() {
         return objectCount;
      }

   private:
      double length;      // Length of a box
      double breadth;     // Breadth of a box
      double height;      // Height of a box
};

// Initialize static member of class Box
int Box::objectCount = 0;

int main(void) {

   // Print total number of objects before creating object.
   cout << "Inital Stage Count: " << Box::getCount() << endl;

   Box Box1(3.3, 1.2, 1.5);    // Declare box1
   Box Box2(8.5, 6.0, 2.0);    // Declare box2

   // Print total number of objects after creating object.
   cout << "Final Stage Count: " << Box::getCount() << endl;

   return 0;
}
```

```
Inital Stage Count: 0
Constructor called.
Constructor called.
Final Stage Count: 2
```

Basic Practice Problems

1. Write a program using classes that takes in a name and age from a user and prints that information on screen to the user. Your class should contain the name and age of the person.

2. Assuming that a class is inherited publicly, which of the listed statements is correct?
   A) Public members of the base class would stay as protected members of derived class.
   B) Private members of the derived class become private members of derived class.
   C) Private members of the base class become protected members of derived class.
   D) Public members of the base class become public members of derived class.

3. Which of the following is the default access type for classes in C++.
   A) Private
   B) Public
   C) Static
   D) Binding

4. An instance of a class is also known as _____?

   A)   Function
   B)   class
   C) object

Practice Problem Solutions

1. /* Creating Basic Classes in C++
*/

```
#include <iostream>
using namespace std;

// Class -------------------
class person
{
public:

//Varibale Declaration
  string name;
  int age;
};
//---------------------
//Main Function
int main()
{

    person info;

    //Get Input Values For Object Varibales
    cout<<"Enter the Name :";
    cin>>info.name;

    cout<<"Enter the Age :";
    cin>>info.age;

    //Show the Output
    cout << info.name << ": " << info.age << endl;
    return 0;
}
```
2. Public members of the base class become public members of derived class.

3. Which of the following is the default access type for classes in C++.
   A) Private
   B) Public
   C) Static
   D) Binding

4. An instance of a class is also known as _____?

   A) Function
   B) class
   C) object

Chapter 8 – Inheritance

Object Oriented programming languages which C++ is, is modeled around objects instead of actions. OOO has 7 major components.

These components include:

- Abstraction – This refers to the hiding of details related to a feature but showing the essential features.

- Encapsulation – This is the binding of functions with variables.

- Inheritance – It allows for the reuse of code without being written over and over. This also allows for classes to inherit information from a base class.

- Polymorhphism – This allows for the creation of functions which contain the same name but utilize a variety of arguments. Even though these functions have similar naming conventions the behave differently.

This chapter will focus on inheritance and using inheritance in C++. Inheritance makes your code cleaner and easier to understand.

Derived Classes

A class has the ability to be derived from multiple classes. This means that it can inherit functions and data from various base classes.

A class derivation list is used to define a derived class. It names one or multiple base classes. The form of a derivation list is shown below.

```
class derived-class: access-specifier base-class
```

Access Control and Inheritance

A derived class has the ability to access all non private base class members meaning that the base class members should not be accessible to the functions of a derived class.

The different access types are shown below according to who can access them and in what specific way.

Access	Public	protected	private
Same class	Yes	yes	yes
Derived classes	Yes	yes	No
Outside classes	Yes	no	No

Type of Inheritance

When a class is being derived from a base class, the base class can be inherited in 3 different ways. It can be done through either **public**, **protected** or **private** inheritance. The inheritance type is determined by the access- specifier, which was covered in the previous section.

The most commonly used inheritance is public. Private and

protected are rarely used but are still useful to know. The following rules should be utilized when using varying types of inheritance.

- **Public Inheritance:** When using public inheritance, the key is to remember that everything that is cognizant of the base and the child will also be aware that the child inherits the base.

- **Protected Inheritance:** When you are using protected inheritance one must remember that only the child and its children are aware that they inherit from the base.

- **Private Inheritance:** When utilizing private inheritance, it is more closed off. No one other than the child is aware of the inheritance.

Multiple Inheritances

In C++ a class has the ability to inherit members from multiple classes. The multiple inheritance syntax is as follows.

> class derived-class: access baseA, access baseB....

In the given syntax, access would be one of the following: public, protected or private. The access would be assumed for every one of the base classes.

Chapter 9 – The New Versions: C++ 11

C++ 11

The first iteration in C++ occurred roughly in 1998. Although there was a long wait for it, C++ 11 was approved in August 2011, 13 years after the first iteration. It has been said that although version 11 is an improvement if the same language, it feels brand new.

C++11 is capable of supporting a number of new

functionalities which include the following:

- Lambda expressions
- Delegating constructors
- Deleted & defaulted function declarations
- Null pointers
- Rvalue references
- Renovation of the C++ standards library
    - New algorithms
    - New container classes
    - Type traits
    - Atomic operations
    - Multithreading library

Within this chapter, you will learn more about core functionality and things in C++11 operate.

Lambda Expressions

Lambda expressions can be defined as large or small blocks of executable statements, much like a function, that can be inserted in place of a function call. These expressions are not only efficient but also secure.

Before implementing these expressions, C++ offered the use of member functions, inline functions and function objects. However, those methods were more laborious.

The following example shows how to utilize lambda expressions while programming.

```
//C++11

vector <accountant> emps {{"Josh", 2100.0}, {"Kate", 2900.0},
{"Rose",1700.0}};

const auto min_wage = 1600.0;

const auto upper_limit = 1.5*min_wage;

//report which accountant has a salary that is within a specific
range

std::find_if(emps.begin(), emps.end(),

[=](const accountant& a) {return a.salary()>=min_wage && a.salary()
< upper_limit;});
```

The highlighted statement begins with the lambda introducer, []. The statement between the {} serves as the function to be executed, similar to a normal function. In the example above, the expression is used to determine if the current accountant object receives a salary which is higher than the given minimum wage yet less than the upper limit. As shown above, being that these expressions are only one line, they are much easier to incorporate in code.

The form of a lambda expression is as follows:

[capture](parameters)->return-type {body}

The first item shown in the form is the *capture clause*. A lambda expression has the ability to have external references. This means that it is able to reach variables the from "enclosing scope". In the given example, min_wage and upper_limit is within the enclosing scope.

External references can be captured in two ways. This

includes capturing by copy or capturing by reference. The method of captures is important because it determines how the expression can manipulate the variables. Each compiler converts each expression into a function object.

To convert the expression a number of guidelines must be followed. These guidelines include:

- Morphing the lambda's body into one of an overloaded operator.
- The expression's parameter list also becomes that of the overloaded operator.
- The variables that are captured, are turned into data members of the overloaded operators.

The closure object is a large part of a lambda expression. This is the compiler generated function object.

When a variable is "captured by copy" becomes a copied data member of the variable from the enclosed scope. When a variable is "captured by reference" it becomes bound as a reference to a variable from the enclosed scope. When an item is categorized as a default capture, it is the capture method for all items within the enclosed scope.

The following examples are that of a capture by copy and a capture by reference. A capture by copy is provided below:

```
[=] //capture all of the variables from the enclosing
scope by value
```

A capture by reference is provided below:

```
[&]//capture all of the variables from the enclosing scope
by reference
```

It is easy to tell if a lambda has external references. An empty capture clause denotes that there are no external references. This means that it accesses only local variables to the lambda.

*[] (int a, int b) {return a*b;}*

The lambdas shown below provide an example of a variety of capture clauses.

vector<int> v3={0,8,9}, v4={11,12,14,15}; //This is the new initialization notation in C++11

[&v3](int a) {v1.push_back(a); }; //An example of capture reference. Capturing v3.

[&] (int m) {v1.push_back(m); v4.push_back(m) };

//This shows the capturing of vi and vi2 by reference.

[v3]() //This example shows v3 being captured by copy.

{for_each(auto   y=v3.begin(),   y!=v3.end(),   y++) {cout<<y<<" ";}};

C++11 also allows lambda expressions to be stored in variables just as regular functions and variables are. An example of this functionality is shown below:

auto fact = [](int e, int f) {return e * f;};

The above auto-declaration defines fact, a closure type. It can be called later without typing the entire lambda expression. A closure type is a compiler-generated function class.

int arr{1,2,3,4,5,6,7,8,9,10,11,12};

long res = std::accumulate(arr, arr+12, 1, factorial);

cout<<"12!="<<res<<endl; //

In the example above the factorial closure multiplies the current element's value for every iteration and the value that has been accumulated. The result will be the factorial of 12. When a lambda is not used, a separate function like the one listed below will need to be defined.

inline int factorial (int a, int b)

{

return a*b;

}

Automatic Type Deduction and decltype

In a previous version of C++, version 3, a type must be specified upon declaration. An initializer is often included with an object's declaration. C++11 allows the declaration of object without specifying their types. Some examples of this are provided below:

```
auto x=0; //x has type int because 0 is int
auto c='a'; //char
auto d=0.5; //double
auto national_debt=14400000000000LL;//long long
```

Type deduction is often used in templates when an object is automatically generated. It can also be used when an object type is verbose.

This new version offers a mechanism for capturing the type of an expression. decltype returns the type of an expression.

```
const vector<int> vi;
typedef decltype (vi.begin()) CIT;
CIT another_const_iterator;
```

The primary intended usage of *decltype* is to declare function templates. These function template types depend on the type of parameter.

Deleted and Defaulted Functions

The example shown below is known as a default function.

```
struct                                                      A
{
A()=default;                                        //C++11
virtual              ~A()=default;                  //C++11
};
```

The bolded portion of the code, =default, tells the compiler to create the default implementation.

There are 2 major advantages to default functions. These include:

- Default functions, compared to manual implementations, are far more efficient.
- Default functions also free the developer from defining functions manually.

Defaulted functions also have a counterpart. The opposite of a defaulted function is a deleted function.

The function has the structure:

int func()=delete;

These functions are useful when attempting to prevent the copying of objects. In order to successfully disable copying. The following 2 member functions must be declared.

```
struct                                                          NoCopy
{
NoCopy & operator =( const NoCopy & ) = delete;

 NoCopy ( const NoCopy & ) = delete;

};
NoCopy                                                              a;
NoCopy b(a); //compilation error, copy ctor is deleted
```

Nullptr

Since the inception of the C language, 0 has served as not only a null pointer but also a representation of a constant integer. Nullptr now replaces NULL and the literal 0 which have been used time and time again as substitutes. nullptr is a new keyword that can represent NULL pointers. in other words, wherever you intend on writing the word NULL, you can use nullptr instead.

C++11 introduces the nullptr keyword as the new null constant pointer. The type for this keyword is nullptr_t. This type is convertible and able to be compared to any pointer type. However, it is not convertible to integral types with the exception of a bool.

The following is an example of a program's implementation before the use of null pointers:

void g(int);

void g(char*);

void h()

{

g(0); //calls g(int)

}

After the creation of null pointers with C++11 the same statement block would look like this:

void h()

{

g(nullptr); //calls g(char*)

}

A null pointer is applicable to all pointer types. These include function pointers and pointers to members. Since nullptr is a pointer type it cannot be converted to integer types. Therefore, it can only be converted to other pointer types.

Delegating Constructors

Delegating constructors refers to the ability to chain multiple constructors together or may call another constructor of the same class. An example of these constructors is shown below:

class Z //C++11 delegating constructors
{
 int a, b;
 char *p;
 public:
 Z(int v) : a(v), b(0), p(new char [MAX]) {} //#1The target constructor
 Z(): Z(0) {cout<<"delegating ctor"<<endl;} //#2 The delegating constructor
};

In the example, the delegating constructor is number 2 whereas constructor 1 is the target, which it invokes.

Rvalue References

Rvalue references are another item that is introduced with the onset of C++11. In a previous version of C++,C++3, reference types were only able to be bond to lvalues. These new rvalue references have the ability to be bond to rvalue like literals or temporary objects.

As a refresher, within the context of C, an lvalue is an expression that can on the right or left side of a given assignment. An rvalue, as the name implies can be seen only on the right side of the assignment. Some examples of lvalues are listed.

int c = 47;

int d = 33;

In the example above, c and d are both l-values:

c = d;

d = c;

c = c * d;

*Of the items above, c * d is an rvalue.*

int e = c * d;

This statement is okay because the rvalue is on the right-hand side of assignment

c * d = 47;

This statement would not be okay because the rvalue is on left hand side of assignment.

The reason for the addition of these rvalue references is move semantics. Moving cannot be directly compared to the copying of an object. In moving, the object which is the target takes the resources from within the source. This essentially leaves the source without any resources or "empty". A move operation is generally used when making a copy is unneeded or potentially expensive.

In order for move semantics to be used to its fullest potential which includes taking advantage of the performance gains, string swapping should be considered.

A very basic implementation would look similar to the example listed below:

void basicswap(string &b, string & c){

string temporary = b;

b=c;

c= temporary;

}

The above example can be categorized as basic or naïve because this implementation would be considered expensive. The copying of the string would also mean that the raw memory would have to be allocated. This would also mean that characters from the source would need to be moved to the target. Whereas, the data members are simply swapped when strings are moved. This is also done without the allocating of memory, without the deleting of memory and without copying char characters.

An rvalue reference has similar behavior to that of a regular reference. However, an rvalue reference has several exceptions.

Aside from solving the problem of move semantics it also looks to solve perfect forwarding. Perfect forwarding allows a developer to write a constructor or function and forward the parameters as an rvalue or as an lvalue.

The following code shows the moving of strings which merely swaps two data members. It does so without allocating or deleting memory or copying char arrays.

```cpp
void moveswap(string& blank, string & full){
//pseudo code
size_t sz=blank.size();
const char *p= blank.data();
//This moves full's resources to blank
empty.setsize(full.size());
empty.setdata(full.data());
//full becomes blank
full.setsize(sz);
full.setdata(p);
}
```

In the event that you are implementing a move supported class, a move constructor and assignment operator can be declared. This can be similar to the one seen below.

```cpp
class Ablemove
{
Ablemove (Ablemove &&); //The move constructor
Ablemove && operator=( Ablemove &&); //The move assignment operator
};
```

One thing to note is that the C++11 Standard Library heavily utilizes move semantics. Therefore, a plethora of the algorithms and containers are now move-optimized.

C++11 Standard Library

Library Technical report 1 was first introduced in C++03. With the implementation of this library C++ received a major overhaul. It included a variety of new container classes and new libraries for components like regular expressions, function wrappers and much more. With C++11 came the official incorporation of Technical Report 1 into the standard. This brought with it a number of new libraries.

C++11 introduced a plethora of new libraries into the C++ language these include:

- Regular expressions library
- Threading Library
- Atomic operations library
- A variety of features within the containers library

Threading Library

One notable addition to C++11 is the addition of concurrency otherwise known as the execution of multiple instructions at the same time. C++11 now supplies developers with a thread class which symbolizes an execution thread. This is known as promises and futures. These are objects which are used mainly for synchronizing within a concurrent environment.

Using the new threading functionality is simple and will be demonstrated in the example below. It is as easy as simply adding the threading header:

```
#include <thread>
```

The following example simply utilizes "Hello World", the most basic of programming tutorials.

```cpp
#include <iostream>
#include <thread>

//This function will be called from a thread

void call_from_thread() {
    std::cout << "Hello, World" << std::endl;
}

int main() {
    //Launch a thread
    std::thread t1(call_from_thread);

    //Join the thread with the main thread
    t1.join();

    return 0;
}
```

Run the above code from your machine. C++11 also allows for the use of parameters in a thread. We have the ability to add as many parameters as needed. The following code has been altered to use parameters and presents the given output.

C++

```cpp
#include <iostream>
#include <thread>

static const int num_threads = 10;

//This function will be called from a thread
void call_from_thread(int tid) {
    std::cout << "Launched by thread " << tid << std::endl;
}

int main() {
    std::thread t[num_threads];

    //Launch a group of threads
    for (int i = 0; i < num_threads; ++i) {
        t[i] = std::thread(call_from_thread, i);
    }

    std::cout << "Launched from the main\n";

    //Join the threads with the main thread
    for (int i = 0; i < num_threads; ++i) {
        t[i].join();
    }

    return 0;
}
```

```
Sol$ ./a.out
Launched by thread 0
Launched by thread 1
Launched by thread 2
Launched from the main
Launched by thread 3
Launched by thread 5
Launched by thread 6
Launched by thread 7
Launched by thread Launched by thread 4
8L
aunched by thread 9
Sol$
```

You may notice that some of the results are confusing or mangled. This is because all of the threads happen to be competing for the same resource. This resource is stdout.

These jumbled results can be avoided by using mutexes or barriers. These barriers allow the developer the ability to organize how the threads will share a particular resource.

New Smart Pointer Classes

If you are unaware, smart pointers are currently defined within the std namespace in the memory header file. They are a key factor in the RAII. The RAII, which stands for the idiom Resource Acquisition Is Initialization, ensure that "ensure that resource acquisition occurs at the same time that the object is initialized"(MDSN).

A smart pointer, is also a class template. This template is declared at stack level. It is initialized by pointing a raw pointer to an object allocated by a heap. After this is done, the smart pointer owns the raw pointer. The smart pointer now is accountable for any deletion of the memory that the raw pointer stipulates.

A previous version of C++, C++98, held a smart pointer class. This class was auto_ptr, which has since been depreciated. C++11 brings about 2 new smart pointer classes. This is shared_ptr and unique_ptr. Both of these new components are compatible with other components of the Standard library. The pointers can therefore be stored in standard containers and manipulated with standard algorithms.

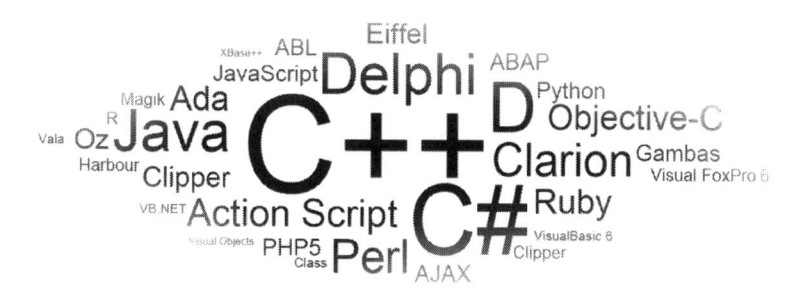

The following definitions have been taken from MDSN.com

and accurately explain the new library components.

unique_ptr

The unique_ptr of the underlying pointer only allows for on owner. Use as the default choice for POCO unless you know for certain that you require a shared_ptr. Can be moved to a new owner, but not copied or shared. Replaces auto_ptr, which is deprecated. Compare to boost::scoped_ptr. unique_ptr is small and efficient; the size is one pointer and it supports rvalue references for fast insertion and retrieval from STL collections. Header file: <memory>.

The diagram shown below illustrates how ownership is transfers between 2 unique pointers.

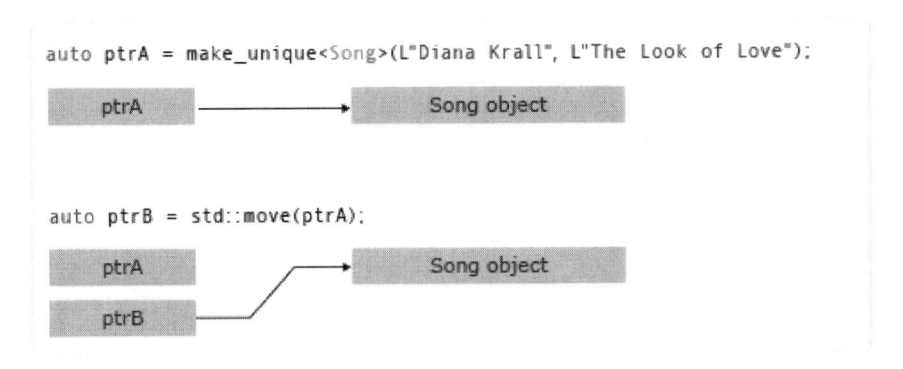

```
auto ptrA = make_unique<Song>(L"Diana Krall", L"The Look of Love");
```
ptrA ———→ Song object

```
auto ptrB = std::move(ptrA);
```
ptrA
ptrB ———→ Song object

The example below demonstrates how to pass and create unique pointer instances within code.

```cpp
unique_ptr<Song> SongFactory(const std::wstring& artist, const std::wstring& title)
{
    // Implicit move operation into the variable that stores the result.
    return make_unique<Song>(artist, title);
}

void MakeSongs()
{
    // Create a new unique_ptr with a new object.
    auto song = make_unique<Song>(L"Mr. Children", L"Namonaki Uta");

    // Use the unique_ptr.
    vector<wstring> titles = { song->title };

    // Move raw pointer from one unique_ptr to another.
    unique_ptr<Song> song2 = std::move(song);

    // Obtain unique_ptr from function that returns by value.
    auto song3 = SongFactory(L"Michael Jackson", L"Beat It");
}
```

shared_ptr

This pointer type is a reference-counted smart pointer. The shared_ptr is used at times when multiple pointers need to be assigned ownership of one raw pointer. For example, when you return a copy of a pointer from a container but want to keep the original. Once all shared_ptr owners are out of scope or have given up ownership, the raw pointer can be deleted. The size is two pointers; the object uses one of the pointers and the reference count, contained by the shared control block uses the other. Header file: <memory>.

The following diagrams shows one memory location with several shared pointers pointing to it.

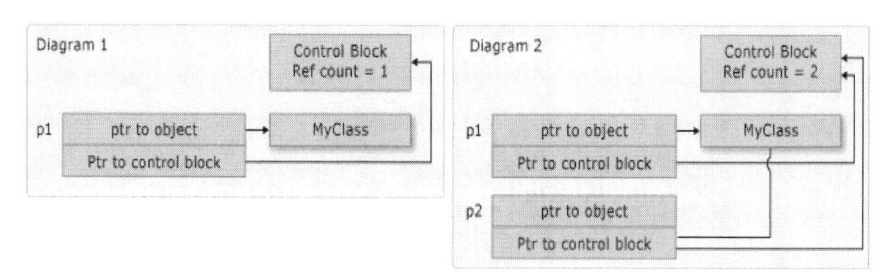

Diagram 1				Diagram 2			
		Control Block Ref count = 1				Control Block Ref count = 2	
p1	ptr to object	→	MyClass	p1	ptr to object	→	MyClass
	Ptr to control block				Ptr to control block		
				p2	ptr to object		
					Ptr to control block		

The following code sample illustrates the declaration and initialization of the shared pointer instance. Once an object as been allocated, these instance will take ownership of the object.

```
//Initialize with copy constructor. Increments ref count.
auto sp3(sp2);

//Initialize via assignment. Increments ref count.
auto sp4 = sp2;

//Initialize with nullptr. sp7 is empty.
shared_ptr<Song> sp7(nullptr);

// Initialize with another shared_ptr. sp1 and sp2
// swap pointers as well as ref counts.
sp1.swap(sp2);
```

Shared pointers can also be passed to other functions. This can be done in the following ways:

- Passed by value
- Passed by reference
- Passed to the underlying object

New C++ Algorithms

C++11 also introduces a variety of new algorithms. 8 algorithms to be exact. These new algorithms include

- all_of()
- any_of()
- none_of()
- is_sorted()
- is_sorted_until()
- is_partitioned()
- is_permutation()

- minmax_element()

All_of, any_of, none_of Algorithms

These three algorithms are very similar. They essentially check if the unary predicate returns true for none, all or some.

```cpp
int numbers[] = {1, 2, 42, 7, 0};

auto is_positive = [](int const n){return n >= 0;};
std::cout << std::boolalpha
          << std::all_of(std::begin(numbers), std::end(numbers), is_positive)
          << std::endl;

auto is_zero = [](int const n) {return n == 0;};
std::cout << std::boolalpha
          << std::any_of(std::begin(numbers), std::end(numbers), is_zero)
          << std::endl;

std::vector<std::string> words = {"to", "be", "or", "not"};

auto is_empty = [](std::string const & s) {return s.empty();};
std::cout << std::boolalpha
          << std::none_of(std::begin(words), std::end(words), is_empty)
          << std::endl;
```

is_sorted()

This algorithm essentially checks to see if the elements within a specific range are sorted in ascending order. The elements within this range are compared using operator<. They are also compared using comp, the binary comparison function.

An example of it's usage can be found below, along with its given output.

```cpp
#include <iostream>
#include <algorithm>
#include <iterator>
int main()
{
    int digits[] = {3, 1, 4, 1, 5};

    for (auto i : digits) std::cout << i << ' ';
    std::cout << ": is_sorted: " << std::boolalpha
              << std::is_sorted(std::begin(digits), std::end(digits)) << '\n';

    std::sort(std::begin(digits), std::end(digits));

    for (auto i : digits) std::cout << i << ' ';
    std::cout << ": is_sorted: "
              << std::is_sorted(std::begin(digits), std::end(digits)) << '\n';
}
```

```
3 1 4 1 5 : is_sorted: false
1 1 3 4 5 : is_sorted: true
```

Is_sorted_until()

This algorithm is similar to the is_sorted() algorithm. It performs the same function by checking if a set of elements are sorted in ascending order however this algorithm returns an iterator. This iterator is to the upper bound which is of the largest sub range. This range is sorted of course. The following provides an example of a program using is_sorted_until() and its given output.

```cpp
int numbers[] = {1, 2, 42, 7, 0};

auto last = std::is_sorted_until(std::begin(numbers), std::end(numbers));
std::cout << "upper bound = " << *(last-1) << std::endl;
std::cout << "sort size    = " << std::distance(std::begin(numbers), last) << std::endl;
```

```
upper bound = 42
sort size   = 3
```

Is_partitioned()

This algorithm does exactly what you would think based on

its name. It checks to see if a range is partitioned. This means, it checks to see if a range is sorted according to a given unary predicate. All elements which do not satisfy the given predicate must be returned after those which do.

The following program is an example of how to use the is_partitioned() algorithm.

```cpp
struct message
{
    std::string text;
    bool delivered;
};

std::vector<message> messages = {
    {"first message", true},
    {"second message", true},
    {"third message", false},
    {"fourth message", false},
    {"fifth message", true},
};

auto is_delivered = [](message const & msg) {return msg.delivered;};

// is not partitioned
std::cout << std::boolalpha
          << std::is_partitioned(std::begin(messages), std::end(messages), is_delivered)
          << std::endl;

// do partition
std::partition(std::begin(messages), std::end(messages), is_delivered);

// is partitioned
std::cout << std::boolalpha
          << std::is_partitioned(std::begin(messages), std::end(messages), is_delivered)
          << std::endl;
```

Minmax_element()

The minmax_element() algorithm finds the minimum and maximum number within a given range. Once it is successfully ran, it returns a pair of iterators for the corresponding elements. Three things we must remember about this algorithm include:

- When a given, range has no values or is otherwise empty, the algorithm will simply return std::make_pair(first, first).

- If there are multiple minimums within a given set of values it will simply return the first one.
- If there are multiple maximums within a given set of values it will simply return the last one.

The function can be seen in action within the following code, with its given output:

```
std::vector<int> numbers = {1, 2, 7, 42, 0};
std::vector<int>::iterator minimum, maximum;
std::tie(minimum, maximum) = std::minmax_element(std

std::cout << "minimum = " << *minimum << std::endl;
std::cout << "maximum = " << *maximum << std::endl;
```

```
minimum = 0
maximum = 42
```

Is_permutation ()

This algorithm is used to determine if one range of elements is permutated from a different elements range. An example of is_permutation in action can be found below.

```
int numbers[] = {1, 2, 42, 7, 0};
int numbers2[] = {0, 1, 2, 7, 42};
std::cout << std::boolalpha
          << std::is_permutation(std::begin(numbers), std::end(numbers), std::begin(numbers2))
          << std::endl;
```

Overall there are a number of changes which were incorporated C++11. So many changes to the point that some consider it almost a different language. You will need time to adjust to the changes. Don't expect to understand them all over night. C++14 brought about great revisions to many of the things introduced in C++11. The next chapter will focus on providing those components and examples of them.

Chapter 10 – The New Versions: C++ 14

C++ 14 was released in December of 2014. It was often coined "C++1y" up until it's release. C++14 added a plethora of updates to the core language. In many instances C++14 builds upon functionality which was added within C++11. Overall it is a much daintier version with less impact on users.

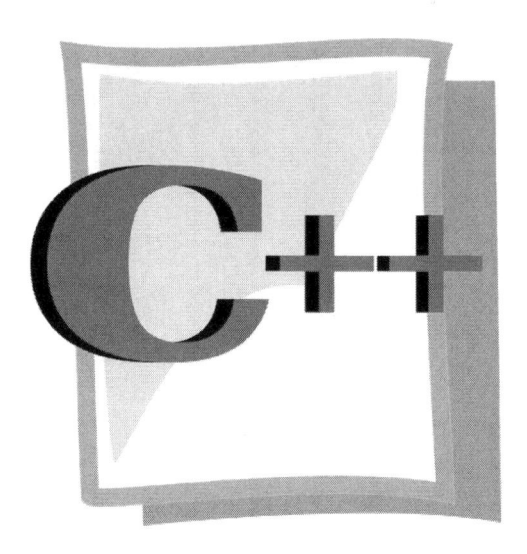

Return Type Deduction

C++11 brought about the onset of lambda expressions and allowed them to determine the return type based on the expression. This newer version gave this ability to all functions. The use of auto is needed in order to determine the return type.

```
auto DeduceReturnType();   // Return type to be determined.
```

Relaxed Restrictions constexpr

C++11 also brought about the notion of constexpr- declared function. This is essentially a function which can be execute at the time of compile. In C++11 a constexpr function could only have one expression.

C++14 decreased the amount of restrictions which were present in version 11. These functions are now able to include the following:

- All declarations except thread_local or static variable types or any declarations without initialization
- Conditions including if statements and switches
- Any loop statements including for or while

The use of *goto* statements has been forbidden in this version of C++.

Number Separators

C++14 now gives users the option of using digit separators. This is simply a single quote used in numeric literals. This includes integers and floating integers.

The feature is anything but earth shattering however it is useful for the reading of numbers. The separator will not change the evaluation of the number and holds no particular coding advantage accept readability.

The sample below identifies how it is used.

```
auto integer_literal = 1'000'000;

auto floating_point_literal = 0.000'015'3;

auto binary_literal = 0b0100'1100'0110;

auto silly_example = 1'0'0'000'00;
```

Keyword: auto

The auto keyword is something new within C++14. Although it was previously introduced in C++3, it now has a different meaning. Its intention is to make coding easier, cleaner and prone to less mistakes. The following is an example of how auto can be used and its equivalent.

```
1    auto i = 1;
2    auto c = return_a_complex_number();
```

The above example is used instead of:

```
int i = 1;
std::complex<double> c = return_a_complex_number();
```

The use of auto also does not have any negative impact on speed. This is due to the fact that auto is deduced at the time of compile instead of the run time. Unlike with in C++11, auto can now be used with functions. You now have the ability to write:

```
auto my_function() {
    ...
    return value;
}
```

Example Programs

The following are examples of the use of the keyword auto in C++11 and C++14.

1) This is the C++11 version of a program.

```cpp
std::vector<int>& add_one(std::vector<int> &v) {
    for(auto& it : v) {
        it += 1;
    }
    return v;
}

void multiply_by_two(std::vector<int> &v) {
    for(auto& it : v) {
        it *= 2;
    }
}
```

The C++14 version is as follows:

```cpp
auto& add_one(std::vector<int>& v) {
    for(auto& it : v) {
        it += 1;
    }
    return v;
}

void multiply_by_two(std::vector<int>& v) {
    for(auto& it : v) {
        it *= 2;
    }
}
```

Generic Lambdas

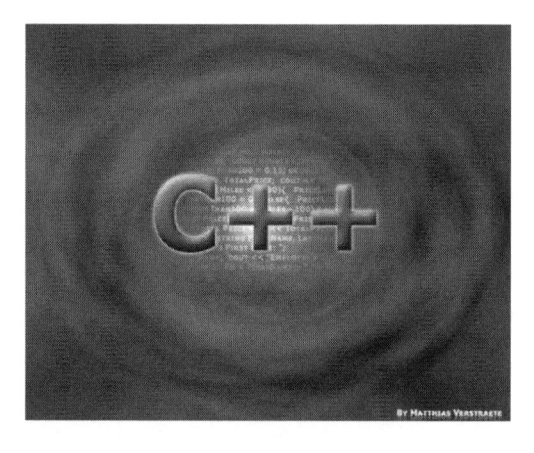

Lambda functions were introduced in C++11, where they needed to be declared as concrete types. C++14 is more lenient in its use of this requirement. It allows lambda parameter to be declared as a type of auto.

auto f = [](auto x){ return func(normalize(x)); };

The above given definition is equivalent to the following pseudo code:

```
class SomeCompilerGeneratedClassName {
public:
  template<typename T>                // see Item 3 for
  auto operator()(T x) const          // auto return type
  { return func(normalize(x)); }

  _                                   // other closure class
};                                    // functionality
```

In the above-mentioned example, the lambda forwards parameter x to normalize. The closure's function call operator is listed above.

In order to correctly write a lambda x must be perfectly forwarded to normalize. In order to do this with the above mentioned code x must be universal reference. It must also be passed to the normalize via std::forward.

```
auto f = [](auto&& x)
         { return func(normalize(std::forward<???>(x))); };
```

Find below a complete program example for the basic use of generalized lambdas.

```cpp
#include<iostream>
#include<complex>

int main() {
    // Store a generalized lambda, that squares a number, in a variable
    auto func = [](auto input) { return input * input; };

    // Usage examples:
    // square of an int
    std::cout << func(10) << std::endl;

    // square of a double
    std::cout << func(2.345) << std::endl;

    // square of a complex number
    std::cout << func(std::complex<double>(3, -2)) << std::endl;

    return 0;
}
```

The result of running the above code is as follows:

```
$ clang++ -std=c++1y -pedantic -Wall -stdlib=libc++ test_01.cpp -o test_01
$ ./test_01
100
5.49903
(5,-12)
$ g++-4.9.1 -std=c++14 -pedantic -Wall test_01.cpp -o test_01
$ ./test_01
100
5.49903
(5,-12)
$
```

New Standard Library Features

With the onset of C++14 come new standard library features. These features include:

- Locking and shared mutexes
- Heterogeneous lookups within associative containers
- Standard literals defined by users
- Tuple addressing

This is a listing of the main library features that C++14

has to offer, there are also a vast amount of smaller library addition.

User Defined Literals

C++14 added a number of suffixes which are used to specify the type of defined literal. Some examples of these suffixes include 's' or 'st'. This is for the character and string type.

```
auto s="Happy new year!" ; ///s is 'const char*' type
auto st="Happy"s ;///st is 'string' type
auto str="new" , str1= "addition"s ;///error
```

The last line of the given example will throw an error. This is because str will be determined as 'const char*' type however str1 will be determined to be a string.

The following suffixes – 'h', 'min', 's', 'ms', 'us', 'ns' are used to signify various time duration interval types.

```
auto sec=60s ;///s is chrono::seconds type
auto hr=2h ;///hr is chrono::hours type
auto mls=56ms ;///mls is chrono:milli-seconds
```

Binary Literals

Up until the advent of C++14 binary literals like 11111101 were not supported. IN order to use them they needed to be converted to a supported type. The following code snippet shows how they are used in programming.

```
//C++14
int x= 0b11111100;
if (var==0b101)
   //...
switch (binliteral)
{
case 0B100:
        //...
        break;
case 0B101:
        //...
        break;
//...
}
```

Binary laterals begin with ob or oB. This prefix is then followed by a series of zeros and ones. A similar syntax can be found in a variety of other programming languages. The programming languages include Java, Perl and Python, all of which already provide support for binary literals.

The binary literal has a type of int. It is accepted in all places that a constant literal is accepted.

Variable Template

The intended purpose of a variable template is to make coding easier and simplify definitions and the use of constants. A variable template essentially is the definition for a group of variables.

A variable template is created by using a template declaration at the place at which a variable is declared.

These are simply a few of the features which were introduced with C++14. A number of other features were introduced but are not strong advancements. Some of the minor features which were included with C++14 include sized deal locations and some syntax tidying. Although the C++14 versioning does not compare to the major updates in C++11 it is necessary.

Conclusion

Congratulations, you have reached the end of this book by learning and applying the things listed in each chapter! Remember that this is only the beginning. In order to truly master C++ you must continuously learn and apply the things you are learning. Now that you have begun your journey with C++ it is pertinent that you stay vigilant.

C++ is a general language that can work with a variety of huge systems, as well as smaller ones. It is a prominent language when creating commercial apps. There are large variety of items written in C++, these include:

- Operating systems like Linux and Mac OS X
- Games like World of Warcraft and the Diablo series
- Popular Wii, PlayStation & XBOX games
- Virtual Machines for programming languages (These languages include Python, Java, Rudy, PFP, Perl)
- Popular software like MS Office, Adobe Photoshop, Inventor and AutoCAD)

- Web Browsers (Chrome, Internet Explorer and Firefox)
- Many Apple iOS applications

This list proves that C++ is a general language that has the power to do almost anything.

If you're wondering if C++ will still be relevant tomorrow or in the next 10 years, the answer is YES!

C++ in conjunction with its predecessor C provide access to hardware and a high level of abstraction. It is the third most used language after C, which falls behind Java as the number one. As of now there is no rival in place to replace C++.

C++ is fast and able to effectively and efficiently use resources. Most fair quality applications are created within C and C++ for embedded systems.

C++ was first commercially implemented in October of 1985. C++ has had continued evolution throughout its life cycle and it follows a distinct set rules. These rules include the following. These rules have been taken from *Evolving a language in and for the real world: C++ 1991-2006 by* Bjarne Stroustrup.

- ❖ General rules
    - o C++'s evolution must be driven by real problems.
    - o Don't get involved in a sterile quest for perfection.
    - o C++ must be useful now.
    - o Every feature must have a reasonably obvious implementation.

- Always provide a transition path.
- C++ is a language, not a complete system.
- Provide comprehensive support for each supported style.
- Don't try to force people to use a specific programming style.

❖ Design support rules:

- Support sound design notions.
- Provide facilities for program organization.
- Say what you mean.
- All features must be affordable.
- It is more important to allow a useful feature than to prevent every misuse.
- Support composition of software from separately developed parts.

❖ Language-technical rules:

- No implicit violations of the static type system.
- Provide as good support for user-defined types as for built-in types.
- Locality is good.
- Avoid order dependencies.
- If in doubt, pick the variant of a feature that is easiest to teach.
- Syntax matters (often in perverse ways).
- Preprocessor usage should be eliminated.

❖ Low-level programming support rules:

- Use traditional (dumb) linkers.
- No gratuitous incompatibilities with C.
- Leave no room for a lower-level language below C++ (except assembler).
- What you don't use, you don't pay for (zero-overhead rule).
- If in doubt, provide means for manual control.

Overall there are a multitude of reasons why people use C++. Simply put, C++ is:

- Flexible – C++ is flexible because it has no limitations that would mandate a certain programming language be used. It can be used in a variety of application areas almost effortlessly.

- Efficient – The fundamental concepts governing C++ mirror that of an everyday computer.

- Available – On all computers there is generally an available C compiler. There are also tools and other resources available so that developers do not need to write items from scratch.

- Portable – Porting items used with C++ is fairly simple and generally feasible.

You have learned the differences between C++11 an C++14, as well as what they have to offer. However, your knowledge doesn't stop there.

To fully gain momentum in programming effectively and efficiently using C++11 and C++14, you must continue to do so. That involves learning, reading and applying these things on a constant and consistent basis. Soon you'll be mastering C++17. Although not yet released, it is important to look ahead and be prepared for what is coming.

Remember each version of C++ offers something new, unique and useful. C++14 essentially built atop of C++11, as it should. It advanced on areas in which version 11 started but didn't complete the job.

Thank you very much for getting this book!

I hope, that you will really enjoy reading it. If you want to help me to produce more materials like this, then please leave a positive review on Amazon.

It really does make a difference!

I think next books will also be interesting for you:

Windows 10

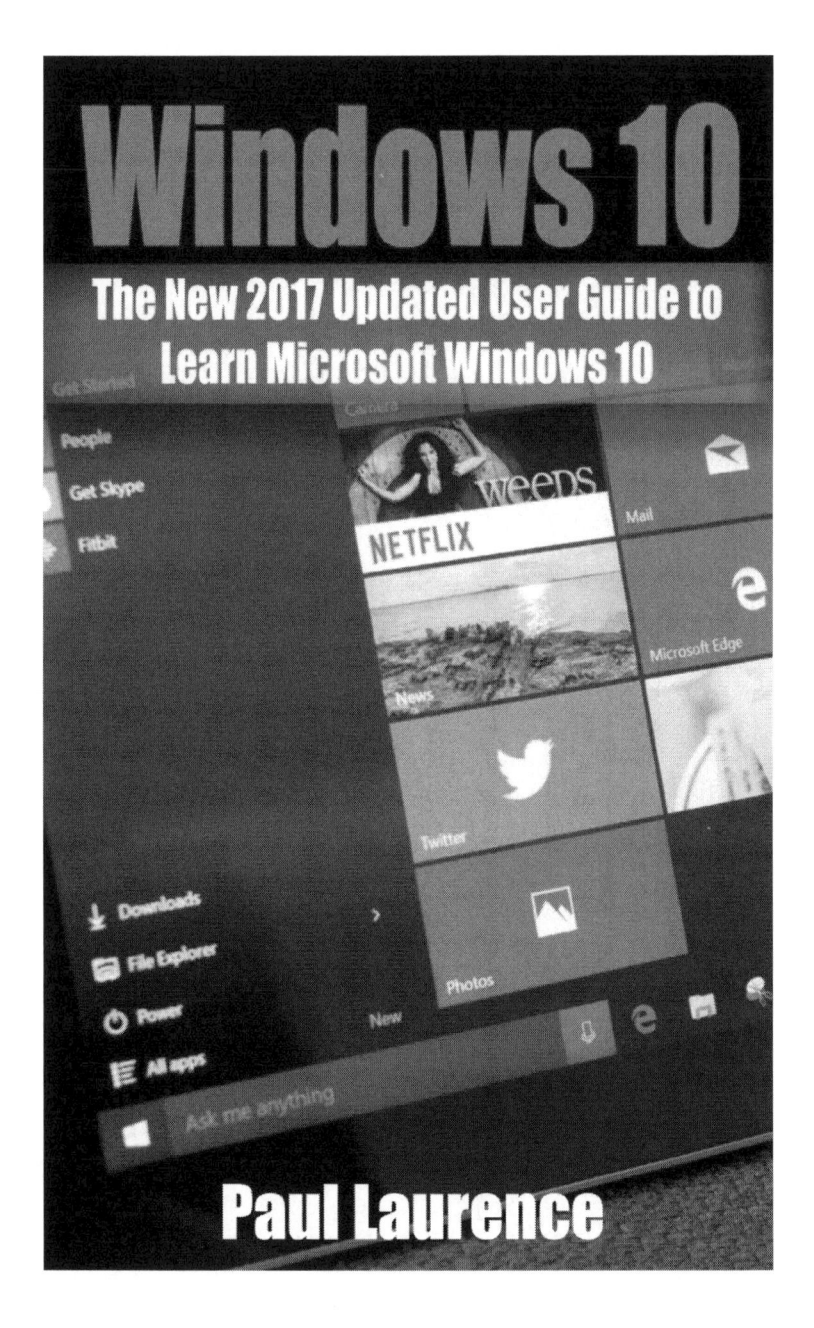

C++

Java

RASPBERRY PI 3

THE ULTIMATE GUIDE ON HOW TO DESIGN AND BUILD YOUR OWN PROJECTS WITH RASPBERRY PI 3

PAUL LAURENCE

Printed in Great Britain
by Amazon